SAINT FRAN

Compiled from the ~~writings and Early Biographies~~
of Saint Francis of Assisi

AUSPICIUS VAN CORSTANJE, O.F.M.

ST. ANTHONY MESSENGER PRESS
Cincinnati, Ohio

Nihil Obstat
Mark P. Hegener, O.F.M
Censor Deputatus

Imprimatur
Msgr. Richard A. Rosemeyer, D.D.
Vicar General, Archdiocese of Chicago
March 2, 1978

The *Nihil Obstat* and *Imprimatur* are official declarations that a book or pamphlet is free of d⸺ nal or moral error. No indication is contained therein that those who have granted the *Nihil (* and *Imprimatur* agree with the contents, opinions, or statements expressed.

LIBRARY OF CONGRESS CATALOGING-IN-PUBLICATION DATA
Francesco d'Assisi, Saint, 1182-1226
Saint Francis Prayer Book.
(Tau books)
Includes bibliographical references.
Prayers. I. Corstanje, Auspicius van.
II. Title
BV245.F67 1978 242'.802 77-28014

ISBN 978-0-8199-0693-9

Published by St. Anthony Messenger Press
28 W. Liberty St.
Cincinnati, OH 45202
www.SAMPBooks.org

Printed on acid-free paper.

08 09 10 11 12 5 4 3 2 1

CONTENTS

Francis was a man of prayer. From the time that he encountered the Lord he was unable to do anything but praise him. He was a living hosanna.

What he eyes saw, his ears heard and his mouth tasted— everything that he smelled, touched, and felt became for him psalm of adoration. "He was always occupied with Jesus; Jesus he bore in his heart, Jesus in his mouth, Jesus in his ears, Jesus in his eyes, Jesus in his hands, Jesus in the rest of his members. How often, when he sat down to eat, hearing…about Jesus, he forgot bodily food.… Seeing, he did not see and hearing he did not hear. Many times, as he went along the way meditating on and singing of Jesus, he would forget his journey and invite all the elements to praise Jesus" (I Cel. 115).

He could not speak without praying and he could not be silent without prayer. His life showed for the power of prayer. It pointed to the risen Lord who is present, who redeemed and liberated us. Francis lets us see that a man begins to live only through prayer, and is able to hope only by entering into the One who lives to pray for us (Hebrews 7:25).

The desert father Evagrius Ponticus declared that anyone who prayed was a theologian. In this sense, then, Francis was a gifted theologian. He never allowed himself to be led by the worldly wise. That is why he was able to rejoice with Jesus: "I thank you, Father,…because you have hidden these things from the wise and the intelligent and have revealed them to infants" (Matthew 11:25).

Francis' life should really be described by means of the prayers that marked out that life.

It was only about thirty years after his death that the first collection of his writings was made, in a manuscript that is still in existence. In recent years, historians have examined the existing collections very closely and we now know which of the prayers were written or dictated by Francis himself.

In addition, a number of occasional prayers by Francis can be found in the early biographies. Their authenticity is dependent on the reliability of these biographies. Examples of these prayers are given in this book, because in our opinion they are very characteristic of Francis at prayer.

—*A. van Corstanje*, O.F.M.

THE LORD OR THE SERVANT

At the beginning of his conversion, while he was still seeking glory and wanted to join Walter of Brienne's army, Francis heard the Lord speaking to him one night.

Now it happened that, after the start for Apulia, Francis felt unwell on arriving at Spoleto; and thinking with apprehension about the journey, he went to bed; but, half asleep, he heard a voice calling and asking him whither he was bound. He replied, telling of his plan. Then he who had previously appeared to him in sleep spoke these words:

"Who do you think can best reward you, the Master or the servant?"

"The Master," answered Francis.

"Then why do you leave the Master for the servant, the rich Lord for the poor man?"

Francis replied, "O Lord, what do you wish me to do?"

"Return to your own place," he was bidden, "and you will be told what to do. You must interpret your vision in a different sense. The arms and palace you saw are intended for other knights than those you had in mind; and your principality too will be of another order."

While he was walking near the church of San Damiano, an inner voice bade him go in and pray. He obeyed, and kneeling before an image of the crucified Savior, he began to pray most devoutly. A tender, compassionate voice then spoke to him:

"Francis, do you not see that my house is falling into ruin? Go, and repair it for me."

Trembling and amazed, Francis replied:

"Gladly I will do so, O Lord."

He had understood that the Lord was speaking of the very church which, on account of its age, was indeed falling into ruin.

OUR FATHER IN HEAVEN

In the lawsuit before Bishop Guido, Francis gave his clothes and all his money back to his father, Pietro Bernardone. Then he prayed in public, deeply moved by the Spirit:

Listen all of you and mark my words. Hitherto I have called Peter Bernardone my father; but because I am resolved to serve God I return to him the money on account of which he was so perturbed, and also the clothes I wore which are his; and from now on I will say "Our Father who are in heaven," and not "Father Peter Bernardone."

PRAYER FOR LIGHT

After the crucified Lord had told him "Go and repair my house," Francis said the following prayer:

Most high and glorious God, lighten the darkness of my heart and give me sound faith, firm hope, and perfect love. Let me, Lord, have the right feelings and knowledge, so that I can carry out the task that you have given me in truth.

In the letter which Francis wrote for a general chapter and for all the friars toward the end of his life, he concluded his exhortations with the following prayer:

Almighty, eternal, just and merciful God, grant us in our misery that we may do for your sake alone what we know you want us to do, and always want what pleases you; so that, cleansed and enlightened interiorly, and fired with the ardor of the Holy Spirit, we may be able to follow in the footsteps of your Son, our Lord Jesus Christ, and so make our way to you, Most High, by your grace alone, you who live and reign in perfect Trinity and simple Unity, and are glorified, God all-powerful, for ever and ever. Amen.

WE ADORE YOU

God inspired me with such faith in his churches [Saint Francis tells us in his Testament] that I used to pray with all simplicity, saying:

"We adore you, Lord Jesus Christ, here and in all your churches in the whole world, and we bless you, because by your holy cross you have redeemed the world."

MY GOD AND MY ALL

My God and my all! Who are you, O God most dear, and who am I, your worthless, useless, little worm of a servant!

Most holy Lord, I should like to love you. Dearest God, I should like to love you. O Lord God, I have given up to you all my heart and my body; and I yearn passionately to do still more for love of you, if only I knew how.

PRAYER IN TEMPTATION

At one time there was sent to the holy father a most serious temptation of the spirit, of course, for the increase of his crown. He was in anguish as a result; and filled with sorrows, he tormented and tortured his body, he prayed and he wept bitterly. After being thus assailed for several years, he was praying one day at St. Mary of the Portiuncola when he heard a voice within his spirit saying:

"Francis, if you have faith like a mustard seed, you will say to this mountain, 'Remove from here and it will remove.'"

The saint replied:

"Lord, what mountain do you want me to remove?"

And again he heard:

"The mountain is your temptation."

And weeping, Francis said:

"Let it be unto me, Lord, as you have said."

Immediately all the temptation was driven out, and he was made free and put completely at peace within himself.

When Francis returned from his private prayers, through which he was changed almost into another man, he tried with all his strength to conform himself to others, lest, if the inner fire were apparent to others, he should lose what he had gained under the glow of human favor. Often too he spoke things like these to his familiar friends:

"When a servant of God is praying and is visited by a new consolation from the Lord, he should, before he comes away from his prayer, raise his eyes to heaven and with hands joined say to the Lord: 'This consolation and sweetness you have sent from heaven, Lord, to me, an unworthy sinner, and I return it to you so you may keep it for me, for I am a robber of your treasure.'

"And again: 'Lord, take your good things away from me in this world and keep them for me in the life to come.'

"Thus," he said, "he ought to speak. And when he comes away from prayer, he should show himself to others as poor and as a sinner, as though he had attained no new grace."

For he would say: "It happens that a person loses something precious for the sake of some trifling reward and easily provokes him, who gives, not to give again."

PRAISES OF THE VIRTUES

Hail, Queen Wisdom! The Lord save you
  with your sister, pure, holy Simplicity.
Lady Holy Poverty, God keep you,
  with your sister, holy Humility.
Lady Holy Love, God keep you,
  with your sister, holy Obedience.
All holy virtues,
    God keep you,
    God, from whom you proceed and come.
In all the world there is not a man
  who can possess any one of you
without first dying to himself.
The man who practises one and does not offend
    against the others possesses all;
The man who offends against one,
    possesses none and violates all.
Each and every one of you
    puts vice and sin to shame.
Holy Wisdom puts Satan
    and all his wiles to shame.
Pure and holy Simplicity puts
  all the learning of this world,
  all the natural wisdom, to shame.

Holy Poverty puts to shame
    all greed, avarice,
    and all the anxieties of this life.
Holy Humility puts pride to shame,
    and all the inhabitants of this world
    and all that is in the world.
Holy Love puts to shame all
    the temptations of the devil
    the flesh and all natural fear.
Holy Obedience puts to shame
    all natural and selfish desires.
It mortifies our lower nature
    and makes it obey the spirit
    and our fellow men.
Obedience subjects a man
    to everyone on earth,
And not only to men,
    but to all the beasts as well
    and to the wild animals,
    So that they can do what they like
    with him, as far as God allows.

HYMN TO THE HOLY VIRGIN

I greet you, Lady, holy Queen
    holy Mary, Mother of God,
    Virgin who became the Church,
    chosen by the most holy Father
    of heaven;
    consecrated to holiness
    through his most holy and beloved
    Son and the Holy Spirit,
    the Comforter;
    in you was and is
    the whole fullness of grace
    and everything that is good.
I greet you, his princely dwelling.
I greet you, the tent of his covenant.
I greet you, his habitation.
I greet you, his garment.
I greet you, his handmaid.
I greet you, his mother,
    with all holy virtues, which
    through the grace and light of the
    Holy Spirit descend unto the hearts
    of believers.
    to make believers of unbelievers
    for God.

O HOLY MOTHER

O holy Mother, sweet and fair to see,
    for us beseech the King, your dearest Son, our Lord
    Jesus Christ, to death for us delivered:
That in his pitying clemency, and by virtue of his most holy
      Incarnation, and bitter death,
He may pardon our sins. Amen.

13

THE POWER OF LOVE

May the power of your love, O Lord, fiery and sweet as honey, wean my heart from all that is under heaven, so that I may die for love of your love, you who were so good as to die for love of my love.

·
·
·
·
·
·
·
·
·
·
·
·
·

Saint Francis began to taste and feel more abundantly the sweetness of divine contemplation and divine visitations.

Among others he had one which immediately preceded and prepared him for the imprinting of the Stigmata, in this way. the day before the feast of the cross in September, while Saint Francis was praying secretly in his cell, an angel appeared to him and said on God's behalf:

"I encourage you and urge you to prepare and dispose yourself humbly to receive with all patience what God wills to do in you."

Saint Francis answered:

"I am prepared to endure patiently whatever my Lord wants to do to me."

And after he said this, the angel departed.

The next day came, that is, the feast of the cross. And Saint Francis, sometime before dawn, began to pray outside the entrance of his cell, turning his face toward the east. And he prayed in this way:

"My Lord Jesus Christ, I pray you to grant me two graces before I die: the first is that during my life I may feel in my soul and in my body, as much as possible, that pain which you, dear Jesus, sustained in the hour of your most bitter Passion. The second is that I may feel in my heart, as much as possible, that excessive love with which you, O Son of God, were inflamed in willingly enduring such suffering for us sinners."

Our Father: Most holy, our Creator and Redeemer, our savior and our Comforter.

Who art in heaven: In the angels and the saints. You give them light so that they may have knowledge, because you, Lord, are light. You inflame them so that they may love, because you, Lord, are love. You live continually in them and you fill them so that they may be happy, because you, Lord are the supreme good, the eternal good, and it is from you all good comes, and without you there is no good.

Hallowed be thy name: May our knowledge of you become ever clearer, so that we may realize the extent of your benefits, the steadfastness of your promises, the sublimity of your majesty and the depth of your judgments.

Thy kingdom come: So that you may reign in us by your grace and bring us to your kingdom, where we shall see you clearly, love you perfectly, be happy in your company and enjoy you for ever.

Thy will be done on earth as it is in heaven: That we may love you with our whole heart by always thinking of you; with our whole mind by directing our whole intention toward you and seeking your glory in everything; and with all our strength by spending all our energies and affections of soul and body in the service of your love alone. And may we love our neighbors as ourselves, encouraging them all to love you as best we can, rejoicing at the good fortune of others, just as if it were our own, and sympathizing with their misfortunes, while giving offense to no one.

Give us this day our daily bread: Your own beloved son, our Lord Jesus Christ to remind us of the love he showed for us and to help us understand and appreciate it and everything that he did or said or suffered.

And forgive us our trespasses: In your infinite mercy, and by the power of the Passion of your Son, our Lord Jesus Christ, together with the merits and the intercession of the Blessed Virgin Mary and all your saints.

As we forgive those who trespass against us: And if we do not forgive perfectly, Lord, make us forgive perfectly, so that we may really love our enemies for love of you, and pray fervently to you for them, returning no one evil for evil, anxious only to serve everybody in you.

And lead us not into temptation: Hidden or obvious, sudden or unforeseen.

But deliver us from evil: Present, past or future. Amen.

LITANY OF PRAISE

Francis composed this antiphon and used it in prayer at all times of day and night and before the Office of the Blessed Virgin. He began with his paraphrase of the Our Father and then went on to this antiphon.

"Holy, holy, holy, the Lord God Almighty, who was, and who is, and who is coming" (Revelation 4:8).

R/. Let us praise and glorify him forever.

"Worthy are you, O Lord our God, to receive glory and honor and power" (Revelation 4:11).

R/. Let us praise and glorify him forever.

"Worthy is the Lamb who was slain to receive power and divinity and wisdom and strength and honor and glory and blessing"(Revelation 5:12).

R/. Let us praise and glorify him forever.

Let us bless the Father and the Son and the Holy Spirit.

R/. Let us praise and glorify him forever.

"Bless the Lord, all you works of the Lord" (Daniel 3:57).

R/. Let us praise and glorify him forever.

Praise our God, all you his servants,

 and you who fear him,

the small and the great" (Revelation 19:5).

R/. Let us praise and glorify him forever.

Praise him in his glory heaven and earth, "and every creature that is in heaven and on the earth and under the earth, and such as are on the sea, and all that are in them" (Revelation 5:13).

R/. Let us praise and glorify him forever.

Glory be to the Father, and to the Son, and to the Holy Spirit.

R/. Let us praise and glorify him forever.

As it was in the beginning, is now, and ever shall be, world without end. Amen.

R/. Let us praise and glorify him forever.

Prayer

All-powerful, all holy, most high and supreme God, sovereign good, all good, every good, you who alone are good, it is to you we must give all praise, all glory, all thanks, all honor, all blessing; to you we must refer all good always. Amen.

As an antiphon for each psalm in his Office of the Passion, Francis recited the prayer to the Blessed Virgin Mary which follows:

Holy Virgin Mary, among all the women of the world there is none like you.

You are the daughter and handmaid of the most high King and Father of heaven.

You are the mother of our most holy Lord Jesus Christ.

You are the spouse of the Holy Spirit.

Pray for us, with Saint Michael the archangel and all the powers of heaven and all the saints, to your most holy and beloved Son, our Lord and Master.

The psalms which follow were compiled by Francis in honor and praise of the Lord's Passion and to commemorate his sufferings. He knew his Psalter well.

Compline
With the Lord, we once again experience his struggle with death in Gethsemane, where he looked to the Father for support, while his enemies were conspiring and his friends were betraying or leaving him.

My wanderings you have counted; my tears are stored in your flask; are they no recorded in your book? (55:9).

All my foes whisper together against me (40:8) and take counsel together (70:10).

They repaid me evil for good and hatred for my love (108:5).

In return for my love they slandered me, but I prayed (108:4).

My holy Father, King of heaven and earth, be not far from me, for I am in distress; be near, for I have no one to help me (21:12).

Then do my enemies turn back, when I call upon you; now I know that God is with me (55:10).

My friends and my companions stand back because of my affliction (37:12).

You have taken my friends away from me; you have made me an abomination to them; I am imprisoned, and I cannot escape (87:9).

Holy Father, be not far from me; *O my God,* hasten to aid me (1:20).

Make haste to help me, O Lord my salvation! (37:23).

Glory be to the Father, etc.

Matins

During the night when he was taken prisoner, Jesus prayed fervently to the Father. He expressed his trust in God, while his enemies were plotting to kill him.

O Lord, my God, by day I cry out, at night I clamor in your presence. Let my prayer come before you; incline your ear to my call for help (87:2–3).

Come and ransom my life; as an answer for my enemies, redeem me (68:19).

You have been my guide since I was first formed, my security at my mother's breast. To you I was committed at birth, from my mother's womb you are my God. Be not far from me (21:10–12).

You know my reproach, my shame and my ignominy; before you are all my foes.

Insult has broken my heart, and I am weak; I looked for

sympathy, but there was none; for comforters, and I found none (68:20–21).

O God, the haughty have risen up against me, and the company of fierce men seeks my life, nor do they set you before their eyes (85:14).

I am numbered with those who go down into the pit; I am a man without strength.

My couch is among the dead (87:23).

Prime
With the coming of dawn, the Lord became sure that God would give him strength. He got himself ready to praise God for this.

Have pity on me, O God; have pity on me, for in you I take refuge. In the shadow of your wings I take refuge, till harm pass by.

I call to *my most Holy Father,* the Most High, to God, my benefactor.

May he send from heaven and save me; may he make those a reproach who trample upon me (56:2–4).

He rescued me from my mighty enemy and from my foes, who were too powerful for me (17:8).

They have prepared a net for my feet; they have bowed me down; they have dug a pit before me, but they fall into it.

My heart is steadfast, O God; my heart is steadfast; I will sing and chant praise.

Awake, O my soul; wake, lyre and harp! I will wake the dawn.

I will give thanks to you among the people, O Lord, I will chant your praise among nations.

For your kindness towers to the heavens, and your faithfulness to the skies.

Be exalted above the heavens, O God; above all the earth be your glory! (56:7–12).

Terce
On the morning of Good Friday, a great hostility toward Jesus was unleashed—feelings were secretly stirred up, justice became a sham, false witness was presented and Jesus was mocked and bullied by the soldiers. Pilate called stridently for his death. In this psalm, Jesus is seen as worthy of our pity.

Have pity on me, O God, for men trample upon me; all the day they press their attack against me.

My adversaries trample upon me all the day; yes, many fight against me (55:2–3).

All my foes whisper together against me; against me they imagine the worst (40:8).

They who keep watch against my life take counsel together (70:10).

When they leave they speak to the same purpose (40:7).

All who see me scoff at me; the mock me with parted lips, they wag their heads (21:8).

But I am a worm, not a man; the scorn of men, despised by the people (21:7).

For all my foes I am an object of reproach, a laughingstock to my neighbors, and a dread to my friends (30:12).

Holy Father, be not far from me; hasten to my aid (21:20).

Make haste to help me, O Lord my salvation! (37:23).

Sext

This is the time that commemorates Jesus' condemnation and the way of the cross. The humiliation of the Lord has reached its peak. The net is gathered more tightly around him. He is surrounded on all sides by hatred. There is no way out for him—he can only go to the Father. He has faithfully endured all this to do the Father's will.

With a loud voice I cry out to the Lord; with a loud voice I beseech the Lord.

My complaint I pour out before him; before him I lay bare my distress.

When my spirit is faint within me, you know my path.

In the way along which I walk they have hid a trap for me.

I look to the right to see, but there is no one who pays heed.

I have lost all means of escape; there is no one who cares for my life (141:2–5).

Since for your sake I bear insult, and shame covers my face, I have become an outcast to my brothers, a stranger to my mother's sons.

Because, *Holy Father,* zeal for your house consumes me, and the insults of those who blaspheme you fall upon me (68:8–10).

Yet when I stumbled they were glad and gathered together; they gathered together striking me unawares (34:15).

Those outnumber the hairs of my head who hate me without cause. Too many for my strength are they who wrongfully are my enemies. Must I restore what I did not steal? (68:5).

Unjust witnesses have risen up; things I knew not of, they lay to my charge. They have repaid me evil for good, bringing bereavement to my soul (34:11–12).

Those who repay evil for good harass me for pursuing good (37:21).

You are my most holy Father, my King and my God.

Make haste to help me, O Lord my salvation! (37:23)

None

Jesus is hanging on the cross. He speaks to us of his final ordeal. The Father seems to be absent at this time. But Jesus only has to pass through death to find him again in glory and to know that the Father has never ceased to lead him by the hand to the victory that is the source of all salvation for all men. The striking contrast between the two parts of this psalm—the second half begins with the words: "When I lie down in sleep"—does full justice to the whole mystery of Easter.

O all you who pass by the way, attend and see if there be any sorrow like to my sorrow (Lamentations 1:12)

Indeed, many dogs surround me, a pack of evildoers closes in upon me (21:17).

They look on and gloat over me; they divide my garments among them, and for my vesture they cast lots (21:18–19).

They have pierced my hands and my feet; I can count all my bones (21:17–18).

They open their mouths against me like ravening and roaring lions (21:14).

I am like water poured out; all my bones are racked. My heart has become like wax melting away within my bosom.

My throat is dried up like baked clay, my tongue cleaves to my jaws (21:15–16).

They put gall in my food, and in my thirst they gave me vinegar to drink (68:22).

To the dust of death you have brought me down (21:16).

For they kept after him whom you smote, and added to the pain of him you wounded (68:27).

When I lie down in sleep, I wake again, *and my Father, most holy, has raised me up in glory* (3:6).

Holy Father, with your counsel you guide me, and in the end you will receive me in glory.

Whom else have I in heaven? And when I am with you, the earth delights me not (72:24–25).

Desist! And confess that I am God, exalted among the nations, exalted upon the earth (45:11).

But the Lord redeems the lives of his servants *with his own most precious blood;* no one incurs guilt who takes refuge in him (33:23).

He comes to rule the world with justice and the peoples with his constancy (95:13).

Vespers

With this hour, Francis' meditation on the mystery of Easter ends. All people and the whole of creation are invited to sing a song of praise to God in response to the wonderful work of redemption. That work is crowned with the Lord's ascension, which was the beginning of his universal reign—in expectation of his glorious second coming before the last judgment.

All you peoples, clap your hands, shout to God with cries of gladness,

For the Lord, the Most High, the awesome, is the great king over all the earth (46:2–3).

The Father of heaven, most holy, our King, sent his beloved Son from on high before all the ages, the doer of saving deeds on earth (73:12).

Let the heavens be glad and the earth rejoice; let the sea and what fills it resound; let the plains be joyful and all that is in them (95:11).

Sing to the Lord a new song; sing to the Lord, all you lands (95:1).

For great is the Lord and highly to be praised; awesome is he, beyond all gods (95:4).

Give to the Lord, you families of nations, give to the Lord glory and praise; give to the Lord the glory due his name! (95:7–8).

Prepare your hearts and take up his holy cross; live by his holy commandments to the last.

Tremble before him, all the earth; say among the nations: The Lord is king (95:9–10).

He ascended into heaven, and sits at the right hand of the most holy Father in heaven.

Be exalted above the heavens, O God; above all the earth be your glory! (56:12).

He comes to rule the earth. He shall rule the world with justice (95:13).

Psalms for Sundays and Feast Days

Compline

A cry for help and an entreaty that enemies may be punished. And at once liberation is proclaimed.

Deign, O God, to rescue me: O Lord, make haste to help me. Let them be put to shame and confounded who seek my life. Let them be turned back in disgrace who desire my ruin. Let them retire in their shame who say to me, "Aha, aha!" But may all who seek you exult and be glad in you. And may those who love your salvation say ever, "God be glorified!" But I am afflicted and poor; O God, hasten to me! You are my help and my deliverer; O Lord, hold not back! (69).

Matins

An invitation to praise God for the wonderful things that he has brought about and which come to a climax in the victory of Easter. That day is above all the day of the Lord. All people and the whole of the earth turn to Christ, who rises to sit at the right hand of the Father and who will send the Spirit on Pentecost Day, so that his holiness will be communicated to his Church.

Sing to the Lord, a new song, for he has done wondrous deeds;
His right hand, his holy arm, *sanctified his Son.*
The Lord has made his salvation known: in the sight of the nations he has revealed his justice (97:1–2).

By day the Lord bestows his grace, and at night I have his song (41:9).

This is the day the Lord has made; let us be glad and rejoice in it (117:24).

Blessed is he who comes in the name of the Lord; the Lord is God, and he has given us light (117:26–27).

Let the heavens be glad and the earth rejoice; let the sea and what fills it resound; let the plains be joyful and all that is in them! (95:11–12).

Prime

As Easter Sunday dawns, at the hour of his resurrection, Jesus meditates about his liberation by God. He prepares himself to rise from the tomb and to sing the song of Easter, inviting all people to join in the song with him.

Have pity on me, etc. (see p. 24).

Terce

All the earth should sing God's praises. Almighty God, who has brought about wonderful and awe-inspiring things, has listened to the appeal that has been made to him.

Shout joyfully to God, all you on earth, sing praise to the glory of his name; proclaim his glorious praise.

Say to God, "How tremendous are your deeds! For your great strength your enemies fawn upon you.

Let all the earth worship and sing praise to you, sing praise to your name!" (65:1–4).

Hear now, all you who fear God, while I declare what he has done for me.

When I appealed to him in words, praise was on the tip of my tongue (65:16–17).

From his temple he heard my voice, and my cry to him reached his ears (17:7).

Bless our God, you peoples, loudly sound his praise (65:8).

In him shall all the tribes of the earth be blessed; all the nations shall proclaim his happiness.

Blessed be the Lord, the God of Israel, who alone does wondrous deeds.

And blessed forever be his glorious name; may the whole earth be filled with his glory. Amen. Amen (71:17–19).

Sext

The promises that are made at the beginning of this psalm are based on the certainty of salvation—a salvation that has already become a reality in Christ.

The Lord answer you in time of distress; the name of the God of Jacob defend you!

May he send you help from the sanctuary, from Sion may he sustain you.

May he remember all your offerings and graciously accept your holocaust.

May he grant you what is in your heart and fulfill your every plan.

May we shout for joy at your victory and raise the standards in the name of our God. The Lord grant all your requests!

Now I know that the Lord has given *his Son Jesus Christ to judge all people faithfully* (19:2–7).

The Lord is a stronghold for the oppressed, a stronghold in times of distress. They trust in you who cherish your name, for you forsake not those who seek you (9:10–11).

But I will sing of your strength; you have been my stronghold, my refuge in the day of distress (58:17).

None

An appeal for help, full of unshakable trust in God's goodness and ready at every moment to become a song of thanksgiving for God's favorable answer that is already anticipated.

In you, O Lord, I take refuge; let me never be put to shame.

In your justice rescue me, and deliver me; incline your ear to me, and save me.

Be my rock of refuge, a stronghold to give me safety (70:1–3).

For you are my hope, O Lord; my trust, O God, from my youth.

On you I depend from birth; from my mother's womb you are my strength; constant has been my hope in you (70:5–6).

My mouth shall be filled with your praise, with your glory day by day (70:8).

Answer me, O Lord, for bounteous is your kindness; in your great mercy turn towards me.

Hide not your face from your servant; in my distress, make haste to answer me (68:17–18).

Blessed be the Lord my God; you have been my stronghold, my refuge in the day of distress.

Your praise I will sing; for you, O God, are my stronghold, my gracious God! (58:17–18).

Vespers

The whole of creation and all people are invited to join in a song of praise, in thanksgiving for the wonderful work of redemption that God has accomplished in sending his Son. That work was crowned with Christ's ascension, which marked the beginning of his universal reign—in expectation of his second glorious coming before the last judgment.

All you peoples, clap your hands etc. (as on p. 28).

PSALMS FOR ADVENT

Compline

This psalm expresses both the long period of waiting in the darkness of faith and trust in the coming of light.

How long, O Lord? Will you utterly forget me? How long will you hide your face from me?

How long shall I harbor sorrow in my soul, grief in my heart day after day? How long will my enemy triumph over me?

Look, answer me, O Lord, my God! Give light to my eyes that I may not sleep in death lest my enemy say, "I have overcome him";

Lest my foes rejoice at my downfall though I trusted in your kindness.

Let my heart rejoice in your salvation; let me sing of the Lord, "He has been good to me" (12).

Matins

Our expectation is fulfilled beyond all our expectations in the great joy of all the poor who trust in God. The Messianic expectation of the Kingdom of God is fulfilled in the Church.

I will give thanks to you, O Lord, *most holy Father, King of heaven and earth;* that you have comforted me (85:12, 17).

You are God my savior (24:5); I will act with confidence and have no fear (Isaiah 12:2).

My strength and my courage is the Lord, and he has been my savior (117:14).

Your right hand, O Lord, has mightily shown its power, your right hand, O Lord, has struck the enemy; in your plenteous glory you have put down my adversaries (Exodus 15:6–7).

See, you lowly ones, and be glad; you who seek God, may your hearts be merry! (68:33).

Let the heavens and the earth praise him, the seas and whatever moves in them! (68:35).

For God will save Sion and rebuild the cities of Judah. They shall dwell in the land and own it, and the descendants of his servants shall inherit it, and those who love his name shall inhabit it (68:36–37).

PSALMS FOR CHRISTMAS

Compline

An appeal for help and an entreaty that enemies may be punished. And at once liberation is proclaimed.

Deign, O God, to rescue me, etc. (as on p. 29).

Matins

This splendid psalm proclaims the wonderful mystery of Christmas: The heavenly Father has sent us his Son as a sign of his love for us.

Sing joyfully to God our strength (80:2); *cry jubilee to the Lord, the true and living God, with a voice of exultation.*

For the Lord, the Most High, the awesome, is the great King over all the earth (46:3).

Our most holy Father of heaven, our King, before time was, sent his beloved Son from on high and he was born of the blessed and holy Virgin Mary.

He shall say of me, "You are my father," and I will make him the first-born, highest of the kings of the earth (88:27–28).

By day the Lord bestows his grace, and at night I have his song (41:9).

This is the day the Lord has made; let us be glad and rejoice in it (117:24).

To our race this most holy and well loved son is given, for our sakes a child is born on the wayside and laid in a manger because there was no room for him in the inn (Luke 2:7).

Glory to God in the highest, and on earth peace among men of good will (Luke 2:14).

Let the heavens be glad and the earth rejoice, let the sea and what fills it resound; let the plains be joyful and all that is in them (95:11–12).

Sing to the Lord a new song; sing to the Lord, all you lands (95:1).

For great is the Lord and highly to be praised; awesome is he, beyond all gods (95:4).

Give to the Lord, you families of nations, give to the Lord glory and praise; give to the Lord the glory due his name! (95:7–8).

Prepare your hearts and take up his cross; live by his holy commandments to the last.

CONCLUDING PRAYER FOR THE HOURS

Let us bless our Lord and God, living and true; to him we must attribute all praise, glory, honor, blessing, and every good forever. Amen.

PRAISES OF THE TRIUNE GOD

Two years before he died, Francis fasted for forty days in the hermitage of La Verna, from the feast of the Assumption to the feast of Saint Michael the Archangel in September, in honor of the Virgin Mary, the Mother of God, and Saint Michael the Archangel. Then, the hand of the Lord came upon him.

After the vision of the Seraph and after receiving the stigmata of Christ, he sang a song of praise to God, to thank him for the great blessing that he had received. He wrote this canticle with his own hand.

You are holy, Lord, the only God, and your deeds are wonderful. (Psalms 77:13)
You are strong.
You are great. (See Psalm 86:10)
You are the Most High.
You are the almighty King.
You, holy Father, (John 17:11)
   are King of heaven and earth. (See Matthew:11:25)
You are three and one,
   God above all gods, (See Psalm 136:2)
You are good, all good, supreme good,
   Lord God, living and true. (1 Thessalonians 11:9)
You are love.

You are wisdom.

You are humility.

You are endurance. (See Psalm 72:5).

You are beauty.

You are gentleness.

You are security.

You are rest.

You are joy.

You are hope and happiness.

You are justice and moderation.

You are all our riches.

You are beauty.

You are gentleness.

You are our protector. (Psalm 31:4)

You are our guardian and defender.

You are strength. (Psalm 43:2)

You are consolation.

You are our hope.

You are our faith.

You are our love.

You are all our sweetness.

You are our eternal life.

Great and admirable Lord,

    God almighty,

      merciful Savior.

ALL GOOD COMES FROM GOD

In chapter seventeen of the longer and earlier Rule of 1221, after stressing the need of humility in all the friars, especially those who are preachers, Francis adds the following exhortation and prayer:

We must refer every good to the most high supreme God, acknowledging that all good belongs to him; and we must thank him for it all, because all good comes from him.

May the most supreme and high and only true God receive and have and be paid all honor and reverence, all praise and blessing, all thanks and all glory, for him belongs all good and *no one is good but only God* (see Luke 18:19).

And when we see or hear people speaking or doing evil or blaspheming God, we must say and do good, praising God, who is blessed forever.

In his Letter to All the Faithful Francis extols the infinite goodness of the Son of God who assumed a human nature like ours and so became our Brother in order to reopen heaven for us:

How glorious, how holy and wonderful it is to have a Father in heaven. How holy it is, how beautiful and loveable to have in heaven a Bridegroom. How holy and beloved, how pleasing and lowly, how peaceful, delightful, loveable and desirable above all things it is to have a Brother like this, who laid down his life for his sheep (see John 10:15), and prayed to his Father for us, saying:

Holy Father, in your name keep those whom you have given me. Father, all those whom you gave me in the world, were yours and you gave them to me. And the words you have given me, I have given to them. And they have received them and have known truly that I have come forth from you, and they have believed that you have sent me. I am praying for them, not for the world: Bless and sanctify them. And for them I sanctify myself, that they may be sanctified in their unity, just as we are. And, Father, I wish that where I am, they also may be with me, that they may see my splendor in your kingdom (see John 17:6–24).

Every creature in heaven and on earth and in the depths of the sea should give God praise and glory and honor and blessing (see Revelation 5:13); he has borne so much for us and has done and will do so much good to us; he is our power and our strength, and he alone is good (see Luke 18:19), he alone most high, he alone all powerful, wonderful, and glorious; he alone is holy and worthy of all praise and blessing for endless ages and ages. Amen.

The greater part of chapter twenty-three, the last in the Rule of 1221, is an exuberant expression of Francis' gratitude for all the blessings that God in his infinite goodness and mercy bestows on mankind:

Thanks for creation
Almighty, most high and supreme God, Father, holy and just, Lord, King of heaven and earth, we give you thanks for yourself. Of your own holy will you created all things spiritual and physical, made us in your own image and likeness, and gave us a place in paradise, through your only Son, in the Holy Spirit, and it was through our own fault that we fell.

Thanks for the First Coming of our Lord
We give you thanks because, having created us through your Son, by that holy love with which you loved us, you decreed that he should be born, true God and true man, of the glorious and ever blessed Virgin Mary and redeem us from our captivity by the blood of his passion and death.

Thanks for the Second Coming of our Lord

We give you thanks because your Son is to come a second time in the glory of his majesty and cast the damned, who refused to do penance and acknowledge you, into everlasting fire; while to all those who acknowledged you, adored you, and served you by a life of penance, he will say: *Come, blessed of my Father, take possession of the kingdom prepared for you from the foundation of the world* (Matthew 25:34).

Thanks through Christ and the Holy Spirit

We are all poor sinners and unworthy even to mention your name, and so we beg our Lord Jesus Christ, your beloved Son, *in whom you are well pleased* (Matthew 17:5), and the Holy Spirit, to give you thanks for everything, as it pleases you and them; there is never anything lacking in him to accomplish your will, and it is through him that you have done so much for us.

Thanks through Mary, the angels, and the saints

And we beg his glorious mother, blessed Mary, ever Virgin, Saints Michael, Gabriel, Raphael, and all the choirs of blessed spirits, Seraphim, Cherubim, Thrones and Dominations, Principalities and Powers; we beg all the choirs of Angels and Archangels, Saint John the Baptist, Saint John the Evangelist, Saints Peter and Paul, all the holy Patriarchs, Prophets, Innocents, Apostles, Evangelists, Disciples, Martyrs, Confessors, Virgins, blessed Elias and Enoch and the other saints, living and dead or still to come, we beg them all most humbly, for love of you, to give thanks to you, the most high, eternal God, living and true, with your Son, our beloved Lord Jesus Christ, and the Holy Spirit, the Comforter, for ever and ever. Amen.

Thanks through all men and women

We Friars Minor, servants and worthless as we are, humbly beg and implore everyone to persevere in the true faith and in a life of penance; there is no other way to be saved. We beseech the whole world to do this, all those who serve our Lord and God within the holy, catholic, and apostolic Church, together with the whole hierarchy, priests, deacons, subdeacons, acolytes, exorcists, lectors, porters, and all clerics and religious, male or female; we beg all children, big and small, the poor and the needy, kings and princes, laborers and farmers, servants and masters; we beg all virgins and all other women, married or unmarried; we beg all lay folk, men and women, infants and adolescents, young and old, the healthy and the sick, the little and the great, all peoples, tribes, families and languages, all nations and all men everywhere, present and to come; we Friars Minor beg them all to persevere in the true faith and in a life of penance.

With all our hearts and all our souls, all our minds and all our strength, all our power and all our understanding, with every faculty (see Deuteronomy 6:5) and every effort, with every affection and all our emotions, with every wish and desire, we should love our Lord and God who has given and gives us everything, body and soul, and all our life; it was he who created and redeemed us and of his mercy alone he will save us; wretched and pitiable as we are, ungrateful and evil, rotten through and through, he has provided us with every good and does not cease to provide for us.

Thanks and praise now and forever

We should wish for nothing else and have no other desire; we should find no pleasure or delight in anything except in our Creator, Redeemer, and Savior; he alone is true God, who is perfect good, all good, every good, the true and supreme good, and he alone is good, loving and gentle, kind and understanding; he alone is holy, just, innocent, pure, and from him, through grace, and all glory for the penitent, the just, and the blessed who rejoice in heaven.

Nothing, then, must keep us back, nothing separate us from him, nothing come between us and him. At all times and seasons, in every country and place, every day and all day, we must have a true and humble faith, and keep him in our hearts, where we must love, honor, adore, serve, praise and bless, glorify and acclaim, magnify and thank, the most high supreme and eternal God, Three and One, Father, Son, and Holy Spirit, Creator of all and Savior of those who believe in him, who hope in him, and who love him; without beginning and without end, he is unchangeable, invisible, indescribable and ineffable, incomprehensible, unfathomable, blessed, and worthy of all praise, glorious, exalted, sublime, most high, kind, lovable, delightful and utterly desirable beyond all else for ever and ever.

WORSHIP GOD AND HONOR HIM

This hymn of praise, now recognized as one of the writings of Saint Francis, is a mosaic of scriptural texts.

Worship God and honor him. (Revelation 14:7)

The Lord is worthy to receive praise and glory. (See Revelation 4:11)

Praise the Lord, all who worship him. (See Psalm 22:25)

Hail, Mary, full of grace; the Lord is with you. (Luke 1:28)

Praise him, heaven and earth. (See Psalm 69:34)

Praise the Lord, all rivers. (See Daniel 3:78)

Sons of God, praise the Lord. (See Daniel 3:82)

This is the day that the Lord has made, let us now rejoice and sing: (Psalm 118:24)

Alleluia, alleluia, alleluia, King of Israel. (John 12:13)

Praise the Lord, everything that breathes. (Psalm 150:6)

Praise the Lord, for he is good. (Psalm 146:1)

All those who read this, praise the Lord. (Psalm 103:21)

All creatures, praise the Lord. (Psalm 103:22)

Praise the Lord, all the birds of the air. (Daniel 3:80)

All children, praise the Lord. (See Psalm 113:1)

Praise the Lord, all boys and girls. (Psalm 148:12)

Worthy is the Lamb that is slain to receive praise, honor and glory. (See Revelation 5:13)

Blessed is the Holy Trinity and Undivided Unity. (Mass of the Trinity)

Holy Michael the Archangel, defend us in the fight. (Mass of Saint Michael the Archangel)

Near the cell of the saint of God at the Portiuncula there was a tree cricket that used to perch on a fig tree and frequently sing sweetly. At times the blessed father would extend his hand to it and kindly call it to himself, saying: "My sister cricket, come to me."

As though endowed with reason, it immediately got up on his hand. And Francis said to it: "Sing, my sister cricket, and praise your Creator with a joyful song."

Obeying without delay, it began to sing, and it did not cease to sing until the man of God, mingling his own praises with its songs, commanded it to go back to its usual haunt.

It remained there for eight days in a row, as if bound there. But when the saint would come down from his cell, he would always touch it with his hands and command it to sing, and it was always ready to obey his commands.

And the saint said to his companions: "Let us give our sister cricket leave to go now, for it has made us sufficiently happy now; we do not want our flesh to glory vainly over things of this kind." And immediately with permission from Francis it left, and it did not ever show up there again. Seeing all these things, the brothers were greatly astonished.

PRAISING GOD WITH THE BIRDS

One time when Francis was walking with another friar in the Venetian marshes, they came upon a huge flock of birds, singing among the reeds. When he saw them, the saint said to his companion, "Our sisters the birds are praising their Creator. We will go in among them and sing God's praise, chanting the divine office."

They went in among the birds which remained where they were, so that the friars could not hear themselves saying the office, they were making so much noise.

Eventually the saint turned to them and said, "My sisters, stop singing until we have given God the praise to which he has a right."

The birds were silent immediately and remained that way until Francis gave them permission to sing again, after they had taken plenty of time to say the office and had finished their praises. Then the birds began again, as usual.

Once when he came upon a great flock of birds, he saluted them as if they were rational beings, and said: "My sisters the birds, you owe much praise to your Creator. He has clothed you with feathers, and given you wings to fly. He has granted you the cleanness of the air, and sustains your life without labor on your part!"

Meanwhile the birds stretched out their necks to him, spread their wings, opened their beaks, and watched him attentively. And as he passed among them his robe touched them; yet not one of them moved, until he gave them leave to depart, and all flew away together.

ON HEARING BAD NEWS
ABOUT THE FRIARS

When Francis heard that some of his brothers were not living the life of the gospel, but playing the part of ascetics by wearing long beards, he raised his hands to heaven and prayed:

Lord Jesus Christ, who chose your apostles to the number of twelve; though one of this number fell, the rest clung to thee and preached the holy Gospel, filled with one spirit; you, Lord, *in this last hour,* mindful of your ancient mercy, planted the order of brothers as a support of your faith and that the mystery of your Gospel might be fulfilled through them.

Who, therefore, will make satisfaction for them before you, if, though they are sent for this, they not only fail to display examples of light to all, but rather show forth the *works of darkness?*

By you, most holy Lord, and by the whole celestial court, and by me your little one, may they be cursed who by their bad example tear down and bring to ruin what you have built up in the past through holy brothers of this order and do not cease to build up.

ON HEARING GOOD NEWS
ABOUT THE FRIARS

When he heard that his brothers in Spain were living in poverty and alternating contemplative prayer harmoniously with the service of their fellow men, and that they were finding the Lord in their community, Francis rejoiced and cried out:

I give you thanks, Lord, sanctifier and director of the poor, who have given me such joy in hearing such things of my brothers.

Bless those brothers, I pray, with your most generous blessing, and sanctify by a special gift all who through their good example cause their profession to give off a fragrant odor.

GREAT THINGS HAVE
WE PROMISED

In one of his instructions to the friars, Francis placed the following exhortation (and prayerful reflection) in the mouth of a simple but wise preacher who touches the hearts of his listeners.

Great things have we promised, still greater are promised to us; let us keep the former, let us strive after the latter.

Pleasure is short, punishment eternal; suffering is small, glory without measure.

Many are called, few are chosen, to all shall retribution be made.

WHY ARE YOU DISTURBED,
LITTLE MAN?

When the enthusiasm that had gripped the order in the beginning began to disappear, Francis found this a constant stumbling block. Again and again he placed his sorrow in front of the Lord. At the end of a long night spent in prayer, he heard the Lord say:

"Why are you disturbed, little man? Did I not place you over my order as its shepherd, and now you do not know that I am its chief protector?

"I chose you, a simple man, for this task, that what I would do in you to be imitated by the rest they might follow who wished to follow.

"I have called, I will preserve and feed, and I will choose others to repair the falling away of others, so that if a substitute is not born, I will make him to be born.

"Do not be disturbed, therefore, but work out your salvation, for though the order were reduced to the number of three, it will by my grace remain unshaken."

AFTER RESIGNING AS SUPERIOR

A few years after his conversion, Francis, to preserve the virtue of holy humility, resigned the office of superior to the order in a certain chapter before all the brothers, saying: "From now on I am dead to you. But see, here is Brother Peter of Catania, whom I and all of you shall obey." And bowing down before him, he promised him obedience and reverence.

The brothers, therefore, wept, and their sorrow brought forth deep sighs, when they saw themselves, in a certain way, to be orphaned from such a father. But Francis, rising and with his hands joined and his eyes raised to heaven, said:

"Lord, I commend to you the family that you heretofore have entrusted to me. But now, because of my infirmities, as you know, most sweet Lord, I am unable to care for it and so I entrust it to the ministers. Let them be obliged to render an account before you, Lord, on judgment day, if any brother of them perishes because of their negligence, or example, or harsh correction."

When he was suffering greater than usual one time, a friar who was a very simple man said to him, "Brother, you should pray to God and ask him to be easier on you. He seems to be treating you too roughly."

The saint groaned aloud at the words and exclaimed, "If I did not know your complete simplicity, I would never let you come near me again, because you dared to find fault with God for the way he is treating me."

Then he threw himself on the ground, shaking every bone in his body with the fall, although he was worn out from his long illness, and kissing the earth, he added:

"I thank you, my Lord and God, for all the pains I suffer and I beg you to make them a hundred times worse, if you want to. Nothing would make me more happy than to have you afflict me with pain and not spare me. Doing your will is consolation enough, and more than enough, for me."

HELP ME IN MY WEAKNESS

After he had received the stigmata, Francis remained in San Damiano. For fifty days at least he could not bear the light of the sun by day and the appearance of the fire at night…. His eyes hurt him so much that he could not rest and he had practically no sleep. One night, when he was lying there thinking of the misery that he had to endure, he was sorry for himself and prayed:

"Lord, help me in my weakness! Then I will have the strength to be patient."

Suddenly he heard a voice say: "Just tell me, brother: if you were to receive, as a reward for your suffering and misery, an immeasurable and precious treasure—the whole earth changed into pure gold, the rocks into jewels, and the water into perfume—would you not regard the earth, the rocks and the water as nothing compared with such a treasure? Would you not be very glad with it?"

Francis replied: "Lord, that would be a very great treasure, very precious and not to be compared with anything that a man can long for!"

"Well, brother," said the voice, "be glad and rejoice in the midst of your suffering and misery! Live from now on in happiness, as though you were sharing in my Kingdom."

In the early morning, his companions came to visit him and found him drunk with joy despite his pain. Radiantly he declared:

"The Lord has given me strength. Thanks to the Father, the Son, and the Holy Spirit for the grace that the Lord has given me. He has given me, his worthless servant, the certainty of blessedness while I am still in this life.

"I must therefore compose a poem today in praise of God, for our consolation and for the edification of our fellow-men in order to glorify the creatures that we need every day if we are to go on living.

"Men often sin by abusing God's creatures. We forget the Creator and Giver of everything that is good in our unthinking ingratitude."

He sat thinking for awhile and then composed the poem. He said aloud:

"Most high, almighty, and good Lord." Then he composed a melody for the text, sang it aloud and taught it to his brothers.

CANTICLE OF BROTHER SUN

Most high, all-powerful, all good, Lord!
All praise is yours, all glory, all honor and all blessing.
To you, alone, Most High, do they belong.
No mortal lips are worthy
to pronounce your name.
All praise be yours, my Lord, through
all that you have made,
and first my lord Brother Sun,
who brings the day; and light you
give to us through him.
How beautiful is he, how radiant in
all his splendor!
Of you, Most High, he bears
the likeness.
All praise be yours, my Lord, through
Sister Moon and Stars;
In the heavens you have made them,
bright and precious and fair.
All praise be yours, my Lord, through
Brothers Wind and Air,
and fair and stormy, all the

weather's moods, by which you
cherish all that you have made.
All praise be yours, my Lord,
through Sister Water,
so useful, lowly, precious and pure.
All praise be yours, my Lord, through
Brother Fire,
through whom you brighten up
the night.
How beautiful is he, how gay!
Full of power and strength.
All praise be yours, my Lord, through
Sister Earth, our mother,
who feeds us in her sovereignty
and produces various fruits
with colored flowers and herbs.
All praise be yours, my Lord, through
those who grant pardon
for love of you;
through those who endure
sickness and trial.

Happy those who endure in peace.
>By you, Most High, they will be
>crowned.

All praise be yours, my Lord,
>through Sister Death,
>from whose embrace no mortal
>can escape.

Woe to those who die in mortal sin!
>Happy those She finds doing
>your will!
>The second death can do no
>harm to them.

Praise and bless my Lord, and give
>him thanks,
>and serve him with great humility.

Above all creatures unendowed with reason he had a particular love for the sun and for fire. He used to say:

At dawn, when the sun rises, all men should praise God, who created him for our use, and through him gives light to our eyes by day. And at nightfall every man should praise God for Brother Fire, by whom he gives light to our eyes in the darkness. For we are all blind, and by these two brothers of ours God gives light to our eyes, so we should give special praise to our Creator for these and other creatures that serve us day by day.

BROTHER FIRE, TEMPER YOUR HEAT

When blessed Francis came to the hermitage of Fonte Colombo to undergo a cure for his eyes—which he did under obedience to the orders of the Lord Cardinal of Ostia and of Brother Elias the Minister General—the doctor came to visit him one day. When he had examined him, he told blessed Francis that he wished to make a cautery from the jaw up to the eyebrow of the weaker eye.

When the iron had been placed in the fire to make the cautery, blessed Francis was afraid that he might show weakness, and wishing to strengthen his resolution, spoke to the fire, saying:

"Brother Fire, so noble and useful among other creatures, be gentle to me in this hour, for I have always loved you and will always do so for love of Him who created you. I pray our Creator, who made us, to temper your heat so that I can bear it."

And as he ended this prayer, he blessed the fire with the sign of the cross. At this moment we who were with him were so overcome with pity and compassion for him that we all fled, and left him alone with the doctor. When the cautery was completed we came back, and he said:

"Faint hearts! Men of little faith! Why did you run away? I assure you that I felt no pain or heat from the fire. Indeed, if this cautery does not satisfy the doctor, let him do it again."

The most holy Father had now been informed by the Holy Spirit as well as by the doctors that his death was near. Hitherto he had been lodged in the bishop's palace, but when he felt himself growing steadily worse and his bodily powers failing, he asked to be carried on a litter to Saint Mary of the Portiuncula, so that his bodily life should draw to its close in the place where his spiritual life and light had come into being.

When the brethren who were carrying him arrived at the hospice standing by the road halfway between Assisi and Saint Mary's, he asked the bearers to set the litter on the ground. And although his long-standing and severe disease of the eyes had almost deprived him of sight, he had the litter turned to face the city of Assisi. Raising himself a little, he blessed the city, saying:

"Lord, it is said that in former days this city was the haunt of wicked men. But now it is clear that of your infinite mercy and in your own time you have been pleased to shower especial and abundant favors upon it. Of your goodness alone you have chosen it for yourself, that it may become the home and dwelling of those who know you in truth and glorify your holy Name, and spread abroad the fragrance of a good report, of holy life, of true doctrine, and of evangelical perfection to all Christian people. I therefore beseech you, O Lord Jesus

Christ, Father of mercies, that you will not remember our ingratitude, but ever be mindful of your abundant compassion which you have showed towards it, that it may ever be the home and dwelling-place of those who know you in truth and glorify your blessed and most glorious Name for ever and ever. Amen."

As the moment of his death drew near, the saint had all the friars who were there called to his side; he spoke to them gently with fatherly affection, consoling them for his death and exhorting them to love God.

He mentioned especially poverty and patient endurance and the necessity of holding to the faith of the holy Roman Church, and gave the Gospel preeminence over any other rule of life.

The friars were grouped about him and he stretched out his arms over them in the form of a cross, because he loved that sign, and blessed all the friars, both present and absent, in the power and in the name of the Crucified. Then he added:

"I bid you good-bye, all you my sons, in the fear of God. Remain in him always. There will be trials and temptations in the future, and it is well for those who persevere in the life they have undertaken. I am on my way to God, and I commend you all to his favor."

When he had finished his inspiring admonition, he told them to bring a book of the Gospels and asked to have the passage of Saint John read which begins, "Before the paschal feast began" (John 13:1) Then, as

best he could, he intoned Psalm 142 and recited it all down to
the last verse:

> With my voice I cry out to the LORD,
>> with my voice I make supplication to the LORD
> I pour out my complaint before him;
>> I tell my trouble before him.
> When my spirit is faint,
>> you know my way.
>
> In the path where I walk
>> they have hidden a trap for me.
> Look on my right hand and see—
>> there is no one who takes notice of me;
> no refuge remains to me;
>> no one cares for me.
>
> I cry to you, O LORD;
>> I say, "You are my refuge,
>> my portion in the land of the living."
> Give heed to my cry,
>> for I am brought very low.
>
> Save me from my persecutors,
>> for they are too strong for me.
> Bring me out of prison,
>> so that I may give thanks to your name.

> The righteous will surround me,
>> for you will deal bountifully with me.

At last, when all God's mysteries had been accomplished in him, his holy soul was freed from his body and assumed into the abyss of God's glory and Francis fell asleep in God.

PEACE PRAYER

Lord,
Make me an instrument of your peace:
Where there is hatred, let me sow love;
Where there is discord, harmony;
Where there is injury, pardon;
Where there is error, truth;
Where there is despair; hope;
Where there is darkness, light;
Where there is sadness, joy;

O Divine Master,
Grant that I may not so much seek:
To be consoled, as to console;
To be understood, as to understand;
To be loved, as to love.
For it is in giving, that we receive;
It is in forgetting self, that we find ourselves;
It is in pardoning, that we are pardoned; and
It is in dying, that we are born to eternal life.

The numbers of the notes correspond to the numbers given to the prayers of Saint Francis; there is one note for each prayer.

1. Three Companions, II, 6; *Saint Francis of Assisi, Writings and Early Biographies; English Omnibus of the Sources for the Life of Saint Francis,* edited by M.A. Habig O.F.M. (Cincinnati: St. Anthony Messenger Press, 2008), p. 895. See II Celano, 6; *Omnibus,* p. 366. Also Bonaventure, Major Life, I, 3; *Omnibus,* p. 637.

2. Three Companions, V. 13; *Omnibus,* pp. 903–904. See II Celano, 10; *Omnibus,* p. 370. Also Bonaventure, Major Life, II, 6; *Omnibus,* p. 640.

3. Three Companions, V, 20; *Omnibus,* p. 909. See II Celano 12; *Omnibus,* p. 372. Also Bonaventure, Major Life, II, 6; *Omnibus,* p. 894.

4. Not previously included in editions of the writings of Saint Francis, this prayer (in Latin and German) is in Kajetan Esser O.F.M., *Die Opuscula des Hl. Franziskus von Assisi: Neue textkritische Edition* (Rome: Grottaferrata, 1976), p. 356. The English translation is by A. Corstanje O.F.M.

5. *Opuscala,* p. 263; *Omnibus,* p. 108.

6. *Opuscala,* p. 438; *Omnibus,* p. 67.

7. Not in *Opuscala,* but in Bartholomew of Pisa, Liber de Conformitatibus, *Analecta Franciscana,* V, 255. The English translation is from M.A. Habig O.F.M., *Tertiary's Companion,* Revised Edition, 1976, pp. 207, 209.

8. II Celano, 115: *Omnibus,* p. 458. See "Legend of Perugia," 21; *Omnibus,* p. 998.

9. II Celano, 99; *Omnibus,* p. 132.

10. *Opuscula,* p. 427; *Omnibus,* p. 444.

11. Translation by A. Corstanje from *Opuscula*, p. 418. See *Omnibus*, p. 135.

12. Translation by J. Meyer O.F.M. in *Words of St. Francis* (Chicago: Franciscan Herald, 1952), p. 198 and note 233 on p. 336: "Found in the De la Haye edition of Wadding's *Opera Omnia S. P. N. F.*, p. 18; maintained as authentic by P. Sabatier in *Opuscules de Critique Historique*, fasc. X, p. 164." Not regarded as authentic by Esser in *Ospuscula*.

13. Better known by its Latin title, *Absorbeat*, this prayer is in the Quaracchi edition of the *Writings of St. Francis* (1949). It is found in Ubertinus de Casale's *Arbor Vitae*, V. 4, but not regarded as authentic by K. Esser in *Opuscula*. The translation is from *Omnibus*, p. 161.

14. Little Flowers (The Stigmata, Third Consideration), *Omnibus*, p. 1448. There are other short prayers of Saint Francis on pp. 1444-1447. See B. Bughetti, *I Fioretti* (Firenze: n.p. , 1958), p. 238.

15. *Opuscula*, p. 292 *Omnibus*, p. 159.

16. *Opuscula*, p. 320 *Omnibus*, pp. 138–139.

17. *Opuscula*, p. 339 *Omnibus*, p. 142.

18. *Opuscula*, p. 338 *Omnibus*, p. 140. Concerning the question of the rubrics for the Office of the Passion, see Esser, *Ospuscula*, p. 337.

19. *Opuscula*, p. 142, from which the English translation was made by A. Corstanje. See *Omnubus*, pp. 125–126.

20. *Opuscula*, p. 392; *Omnitubs*, p. 45.

21. *Opuscula*, p. 211; *Omnitubs*, p. 96.

22. *Opuscula*, pp. 399–401; *Omnitubs*, pp. 50–52.

23. *Opuscula*, p. 282, from which the English translation was made by A. Corstanje. This prayer was not previously included among the authentic writings of Saint Francis.

24. II Celano, 171; *Omnibus*, p. 499. See Bonaventure, Major Life, VII, 9; *Omnibus*, p. 695. Also "Legenda Antiqua," cap. 76.

25. The first selection is from Bonaventure, Major Life, VIII, 9; *Omnibus*, p. 695. The second selection (in which Francis' sermon to the birds is quoted) is from

the life of Saint Francis by Bl. Jacob de Voragine (died 1298) in his *The Golden Legend,* translated and adapted from the Latin by Granger Ryan and Helmut Ripperger (New York: Longmans, 1948), p. 606. The paragraph which follows tells the story of the birds (swallows) which interrupted their singing at the bidding of Francis.

26. II Celano, 156; *Omnibus,* p. 488. See Bonaventure, Major Life, VIII, 3; *Omnibus,* p. 690.

27. II Celano, 178; *Omnibus,* p. 505.

28. II Celano, 191; *Omnibus,* p. 516.

29. II Celano, 158; *Omnibus,* pp. 489–490. See Bonaventure, Major Life, VIII, 3; *Omnibus,* p. 690.

30. II Celano, p. 143; *Omnibus,* p. 478. See Mirror of Perfection, 39; *Omnibus,* p. 1165.

31. Bonaventure, Major Life, XIV, 2; *Omnibus,* p. 738.

32. Mirror of Perfection, 100; *Omnibus,* pp. 1235–1236. See "Legenda Antiqua," p. 39. Translation by A. Corstanje.

33. *Opuscula,* p. 128; *Omnibus,* p. 138.

34. Mirror of Perfection, 119; *Omnibus,* p. 1257.

35. Mirror of Perfection, 115; *Omnibus,* p. 1254. See Bonaventure, Major Life, V, 9; *Omnibus,* p. 668.

36. Mirror of Perfection, 124; *Omnibus,* p. 1264. See "Legenda Antiqua," p. 90.

37. Bonaventure, Major Life, XIV, 5; *Omnibus,* p. 740. See II Celano, 217; *Omnibus,* p. 536. Psalm 142 (Psalm 141 in Bonaventure), English translation, is *NRSV.*

38. The so-called "Peace Prayer of Saint Francis" was not written by Francis, but it admirable expresses the spirit of "the Man of Peace." For the origin of this prayer, see *Franciscan Herald,* May 1974, p. 151. See K. Esser, *Opuscula,* p. 54. The English version given here has three additional lines which are found in European versions: the French, Italian and Spanish versions add petitions for establishing *harmony* where there is *discord* and *truth* where there is *error;* and

in the second part the French states that we *find ourselves in forgetting self*. The translation, by M.A. Habig O.F.M., is from *Franciscan Herald*, pp. 152–153, where the French, Italian and Spanish texts are also given. See A. Corstanje, *Francis: Bible of the Poor* (Chicago: Franciscan Herald, 1977), pp. 203–211.